Safe Harbor

Margie Wright

Presentation by *BookLeaf Publishing*

Web: www.bookleafpub.com

E-mail: info@bookleafpub.com

ISBN: 9789358312904

First edition 2023

*For my brother, Ponder, who buried me
with all his toys when he was not quite
three and continued to shower me with
kindness all the days of my life. He will
always be Batman to my Robin.*

ACKNOWLEDGEMENT

I continue to be grateful to JD Ballam and Gail Anderson who saved my life by supporting me daily as I battled cancer and the fallout thereafter. When disability robbed me of my future, they saved me once again when they welcomed me to Oxford's Creative Writing department introducing me to tutors Shaun, Claire, Bea, and Elisabeth, who led me to believe my life was just beginning at 60.

And as always, a special thanks to Dr. Robert Droder who salvaged me from the medical lost and found and fought to save my legs, my life, and my place at Oxford.

PREFACE

This anthology is full of cameos of my life's deckhands who have traveled with me as I set sail in calm, pleasant waters, encounter a few storms at sea, and finally make safe harbor within myself.

Oh, Batman, My Batman!

Oh, my brother, you will never know
How I cherish our memories so
Of when you were a little child
Yet so grown up and a little wild

You'd take me to the store with you
I never knew what I was supposed to do
But you were always there with me
So, I was safe as safe could be

If I fell down and scraped my knee
You were the one who cared for me
You took my hand and patched me up
Put an end to all the fuss

You taught me how to climb a tree
So I could join the block's army
When initiation concreted my hair
You helped mom rinse it out of there

You taught me how to be a spy
To wear my bangs across one eye
And groovy is as groovy does
The Spy Out group was quite a club

The attic was a magical place

And magic happened within that space
Oh, there was pain stepping on a nail
And there was blood, that never failed

Momma screamed and
Momma cried
When I fell off the roof
And she thought I'd died

But you told Momma I was tough
I'd proved myself to be pretty rough
I'd earned my wings in Batman towel
And I was ready for bigger things now

I earned wearing your shoulder pads
And played football with all the lads
We became champs of all the block
We became the team they could not stop

When it was time to learn to box
You padded me a big tube sock
And marked an arena out in the yard
And told both girls to swing real hard

When Tammy fell with just one blow
Your pride in me began to glow
But her mom got mad and ran to mine
So, I was golden gloves just one time

But still you were so proud of me
I won a ribbon and a pack of Spree
I was proud, though my hand did smart,
To win the prize of my brother's heart

That was what it all meant, you see
Champions were always you and me
From the beginning, we'd always win
Phenomenal success again and again

You had my back from the very start
And with it came my little heart
You Buried me in toys 'til I couldn't see
From that moment it was you and me

Now we are too old to jump off the roof
Or play football with a backyard group
Or climb up into the attic to be a spy
Or sock neighbor girl in her weak eye

But my heart makes a run to yesteryear
And the days of fun when you were near
Growing up was sort of a bust
Giving up the yard and the team of us

You still throw long-bombs in my heart
You're my best buddy from the start
You're a touchdown without end
Forever coach, Batman, brother, friend

The Gipper

I have a brother big and strong
And he knows everything
And he can box your socks off
And he's got a Super Bowl ring

He's Tom Landry and Roger Staubach
All rolled into one
If you mess with me at recess
He'll clean your clock for fun

You don't know it, but I am Calvin Hill
And he counts on me
To make the touchdown in our yard
For all the block to see

We are champions of our block
And all around the town
He hits me right on the numbers
And I fly over the ground

To score one more for the Gipper
I blitz into the end zone
We don't need no other players
We can do it on our own

What you see ain't what you get
'Cause when me and him suit up in pads
He calls the plays, and throws to me
I play better than all you sorry lads

So if you beat up on me today
And tear this girly dress
My brother's going to whup your rear
You'll leave this playground a mess

'Cause my brother is big and strong
And he knows everything…

Joe

There is a name I'll always know
The precious name of my dog Joe
He was the same age as me
We grew up together
This dog and me

He was black and I was white
He slept beside my bed at night
He kept me safe from scary witch
I would sleep safely
As he'd dream and twitch

He'd wear a shirt for me
And sometimes a tie
I'd put on him some lipstick
And Daddy's hat
Then he would be a spy

He'd eat my biscuits and play dough too
There's nothing much he wouldn't do
He'd drink out of my best teacup
And If I asked that sweet baboo
He'd be the animals in my zoo

I taught him how to read and right

His glasses fit him a little tight
I'd paint a picture and he would too
And fall asleep with paws of blue
I loved that dog with all my might

But one day the angels called for him
And I did too without end
Grandpa said "Listen, Kid, he's dead."
I wept night and day upon my bed
I hated life without my friend

We grew up together, this dog and me
He was my love and will always be
His name is one that you should know
The precious name of my dog
 Joe

The Mailman

I am in love with the mailman
He sits on the third row
And looks just like the other kids
But there's something they don't know

In the Easter talent show
He'll carry all the mail he can
But it's not all inside his pouch
One envelope will hold his hand

They will walk around the stage
And the envelope will be
In a blue dress with a card sewn on top
And that girl will be me!

We shall approach the risers together
Hand in hand we shall be
As the class sings of community helpers
And my postman boyfriend and me

My mom had yards of postal blue
And little pillow addressed like a card
She told teacher I'd be the envelope
And it wouldn't be too hard

So now I hold hands with the mailman
That groovy blonde boy on row three
We leave to go practice for the show
And I am happy as can be

Cause I'm in love with the mailman
Who sits on the third row
Looking like the other kids
But I know something they don't know

Using Me

I lie here awake trying to figure out how you love me when you cut me out of everything. I mean I am not stupid, and I would never let anyone else treat me this way. I would write you a poem, but when we are in public, you don't even acknowledge me. You make it pretty plain that I am cut out of your life every day and every way. All parties. All special occasions. Days you're off. Days you work. When you have nothing else to do. You say it's not me, but I am the one you get mad and refuse to talk to. I am also the one you refuse to see. It's time for me to respect your wishes and stop pretending that I mean anything to you.
Do me a favor. Stop calling me for help. Stop using me when you need rescue. You leave me absolutely drowning and you know it. But you always call for me when the waves swamp you. That's called using someone.
Let's stop all this
Using me.

I Think I'm Done

I've been thinking about this a long time
And I am pretty sure I am done
Not just with the rat finks
But with everyone

I'm done with everyone who uses me
When they are sad or blue
Then turn around and freeze me out
Of everything they do

I'm done with being your little joke
As you laugh behind my back
Thinking I am too stupid to know
When you insult or attack

I'm done with loaning you all I have
When I'm someone you never see
Hard words and condemnation
Are all you have for me

I'm not supposed to tell the truth
About how you've treated me
But it's easy for the world to know
You make it plain to see

You celebrate life without me now
And dodge my very face
And laugh when others come to mock
And put me in my place

You are dismissive, insulting, and cruel
When I am loyal, kind, and true
I don't know why you play this game
But I am through with you

Setting Me Free

I can't tell you how it hurts
I won't tell you how it hurts
I am setting myself free
I'm not sharing myself anymore
With anyone but me

It's been you all along
It was you every time
Who left me in the rain
Blaming everyone but yourself
Inflicting so much pain

I want you to go away
Go away and stay
If you're not my lover or my friend
Walk out the door
Let the charade end

Thank you, but no thank you
Don't step inside my world
Please don't bother me
I am not sharing my soul with you
Now that I'm finally free

Spiderman, The Hope of Paris

You crossed seas with hope in your hands to
Bravely save this precious child of France
And now always in our glad hearts will live
Come dance, forgiving us, here on this night
You man of strength and swift courageous will
Come save our child from our prejudging ways
As we take you into our hearts forever
Stay dear friend among us on our streets tonight
Our fires to fight and souls to keep safely
Our hearts light up the streets for you tonight
Our son, our brother, our best of friends, our life
A man of peace and truth, our son of France
Make us your home and bring to Paris hope

The Storm

I can feel the raindrops coming
Fast and hard and mean
I can feel those raindrops coming
Running in a stream

I can hear the sound of Thunder
Angry, Violent, Mad
I can feel the clap it makes
When everything goes bad

I can smell the wildfires raging
Burning all around
I can smell the smoldering heat
As all my world burns down

I can feel the raindrops coming
Streaming down my wretched face
I pray they flash-flood over me
And take me to another place

'Cause I can feel the storm coming….

Setting Me Free

I won't say I love you
Or take my pretty paper
And wrap you a gift
Like we belong together

I won't sit down next to you
And share my meal
Or laugh at your joke
Or ask you how you feel

I won't look for your face
Or go to your house
Or stop and talk
When you're out and about

I won't say I love you
And perpetuate a farce
Where I'm the joke
And don't realize my part

I suppose there are outsiders
The paparazzi in our lives
That don't know you freeze me out
And shutter your eyes

But I do and you do

And that is enough
What once was between us
Lies in the dust

I won't show you my poems
Or write anymore for you
Sense the love we once shared
Is over, dead, and through

You made your choice
Was it hard at the time?
Did it break your heart
When you chose to break mine?

But I am flesh and blood
Not a mindless cartoon
Love withers and dies
When tossed from the room

Once your heart lived in my heart
There was no better friend
We floated Moon River
Through each turn in the bend

You were my Huckleberry
And I was yours that's for sure
Until you left me at the dock
And stranded on the shore

I didn't tell our friends
Your rep remained intact
So you helped yourself to my fortune
And then you turned your back

I guess I've started getting old
I'm not pleasing enough
What you planned for our lives
Must be costing you too much

Show me some respect
You're Ghosting me, Cowboy
I am not a boob or a beggar
And I can't counterfeit joy

I won't cause you any trouble
Betray or defame
But I'll go on my way
And stop calling out your name

I dismiss you from my life
I'm not your number one
Your dreams of taking my land
Died with Dad so now we are done

I won't say I love you
Or buy a gift from me
This birthday let's just call it quits
And simply set me free

Sour Cake

I don't think I'll eat your birthday cake
First it was too sugary
Then it lost its sweet
Then soured and went rancid
Till I just couldn't eat

Another bite of hypocrisy
Of the games that you play
Pretending we're pals for watching eyes
Then turn and walk away

You don't really talk to me
I just pass the pecan pie
You nod without a thank you
Never look me in the eye

I take my script from your hands
Mark the village idiot off the page
You shine on, Coca-Cola cowboy,
I am done with all your rage

It's time to leave this party
Leave the Hatter to his tea
Slice the cake and pour the wine
But do it without me

I'll pass on that birthday cake.
No thank you, Cowboy

My Sweet Alone

I must have always been alone
Sadly, it is true
I was way too stupid to know it
Till I was through with you

And then I thought back to the rest
Bigots, hypocrites, and bums
Each after something else
They'd grab parts of me and run

Leaving me alone with nothing
Taking the neutral friends
Even slamming my name at church
Until I could go no longer in

I had Jesus and a real good dog
It dawned on me one night
That the most loyal men I ever knew
Were Poppa, my dog, and Jesus Christ

So even though I live alone
I'm happy as can be
With Hemingway and my typewriter
My dog, myself, and me

Alone is much better than you and me
What a comedic farce
I tried to love as you robbed me blind
And swindled away my horse

All I need is a good typing ribbon
And a book on Hemingway
My dog and I will live in peace
Now you are gone to stay

The Escape

Man oh man, you went away
Getting while the getting's good
Dying's a hard way for a man to escape
But you'd done all that you could

And they were all sucking you dry
I wish we would have known
We'd have helped you get away from them
And find a brand-new home

But it was not to be
Cancer destroys your chance
Before you get to live your life
And finish another dance

So, we came and loved you while we could
Surrounded by those kooks
Who couldn't see death was at the door
And shutting down the books

But those of us that knew you best
Stood around your heart
And let you know we love you still
And keep you in our heart

And when it was time, you slipped away
To weep for never more
And finally rest as you deserve
On heaven's peaceful shore

I never saw a thing like that
But I am glad you got away
I'll walk with you and talk with you
Another one fine day

I miss you so much dear friend
But now I'll dry my eyes
For old friends always share
A love that never dies

Man, oh man, you got away
But Cancer's a hard way to escape…

Butch

You're known to be a real tough guy
A rough and tumble sort
But you were so inclusive
and always a real good sport

Neighbors wanted to play with you
They'd always swarm our yard
You were a block celebrity
You held the winning card

But you were friends to everyone
Even that kid with just one eye
Girls played but were not harassed
Just as if they were a guy

You were friends to the underdog
Turned losers into men
And if they'd suck it up
You'd teach them how to win

You didn't shove me beneath the bus
Even to save your hide
More than once you took the blame
And suffered while I cried

Once you pulled me from the road
Stepping in front of a VW BUG
You grabbed my dress, pulled me back
And saved me with a tug

When Kindergarten Valentines
Turned into a bust
I cried and hid my face for hours
Until you made a fuss

About my secret admirer,
A handsome astronaut,
Sending a love letter you found
That the postman had forgot

You taught me to sing like a Monkee
And dance like Elvis too
Best of all you taught me how to fly
And play football just like you

You taught me how to ride a bike,
Turn toothpaste to shampoo,
And sell it to Grandma and Grandpa
To make a buck or two

And when it came time to work,
Janitors at Lamar Tech,
Being about 5 years old
I held the dustpan while you swept

I had a goldfish in a bowl
But one day he up and died
We flushed him singing Danny Boy
You saluted while I cried

When the neighbor's barn burned down
You sent me back to the house
Firemen looked to place the blame
But my name got left out

And when we broke my brand-new bed
Both guilty as could be
You told Daddy it was all your fault
And took my whupping for me

You were Batman and I was Robin
Pretty liberating back in that day
Gloria Steinem would've wept in pride
If she had seen me play

Football as Calvin Hill
Catching passes all alone
Your long bombs took my wind away
But I made touchdowns on my own

And everything you taught me,
No screaming at blood or crying in pain,
Sure did come in handy in life

When I found no rainbows in my rain

You came bravely to my room
Though Cancer was a scary thing
And gave a half-time bedside chat
"We win and win, then we win again!"

I got going when the going got tough
I used your lessons to fight my pain
There was glory because I had guts
I fought like a girl- the one you trained

Then my legs were ruined
I almost gave up the fight
But I got back up like you taught me
Taking what was left of life

They all call you Butch and Big Daddy
Husband, father, boss, and kin
But I call you Captain, Staubach, Coach
Batman, brother, and friend

Oxford Girl

Harvard? I don't think so
I'm sure it's worth my time
But I just hung Oxford on my wall
And that sheepskin's mighty fine

I'm on a roll with my typewriter
I'm writing all the time
My Oxford training is kicking in
I'm loving every line

It's not that I don't love you
Or won't register in the spring
But I am so busy with my life
And doing my own thing

I've wanted to write books, you see,
I told JD that in my interview
I studied Oxford to write printed books
And now I really do

Oh, I know I am small potatoes
My name will never fill the net
But the things I learned at Oxford
I never will forget

So, Harvard, I'm still interested
But I've got some things to do
Let me enjoy being an Oxford grad
Come spring, I'll get back with you

Confession to My Priest

I am sick to my stomach
Upset with myself too
When you were lending me support
I wound up yelling at you

It wasn't nice, it wasn't fair
It wasn't right at all
I was as guilty as those I wrote about
And you hung up on my call

I don't blame you after all you've been
Loyal, giving, lifelong friend
Trying to understand my pain
Supporting me without end

All through college and new careers
When your own life was not so good
You never failed to love and listen
But today I was really rude

You tore a page out of my book
And simply walked away or
Slammed your phone back on its hook
Would be more accurate to say

I don't blame you, you've every right,
To make me stew in my own juice
But tonight, saying I am sorry
Is of very little use

Cause today I ran off my mouth
Scolding my dear friend
Raised my voice and acted like
I mattered more than them

A friend whose money's with her mouth
And travels up hill and down
To help you when you are in peril
Or just need a friend around

You're the best of friends, you see
In darkness you rushed to my door
Driving all night to comfort me
And for Nathan, doing it once more

So tonight, I am mad at myself
I deserve to lay sick in bed
I hurt my best friend's best intent
Brought shame on my own head

Pride came before my fall
And smacked me on the shin
I hope you'll forgive me after all
My buddy, Priest, and friend

Carolyn

You shared New York with me
And then Alaska too
It opened up my world early on
Gave me a proper view

New York was such a blast
A cross-section of humanity
I hung with hookers, homeless bums
And a host of celebrity

The Metropolitan changed my life
I suppose it does everyone
Time in New York renewed my belief
That life should always be fun

Alaska revived me once again
I never felt so small
I nestled into the Juneau scene
And learned to love it all

And now that life is really hard
I reach into my memory
And use the lessons I learned
From Romeo, Jim, and Nikki

Sometimes when I am lonely
I delightfully rifle my memory bank
Reliving my first Alaskan night
Sleeping with my best boyfriend Hank

We drove out to Eagle Beach
And went way out of site
Got stuck in the quicksand surf
After surviving, he gave me a bite

To let me know if we stayed friends
I'd never do that again
And what a friend he proved to be
Until the bitter end

The last summer I sat house with him
A whale sprayed us in the face
While drinking coffee on the deck
He never moved from his place

But he always let me know of bear
They're so cute for goodness' sake
But scary as they can be unless
You've got a dog like Hank

Sitka, Skagway, Taku Lodge
Douglas, The Valley, downtown Juneau
Saint T's and the Mendenhall
It was so long ago

But I keep it all filed in my mind
Each precious little part
Nikki, Romeo, and Brother Hank
Dwell safely in my heart

They call me to rise up each day
To feast on what life can give
Drink in the beauty, find my peace
Search the waters, partake, and live

Sister, thank you for sharing your world
New York and Alaska too,
For I'd have never known these glories
Without invitations from you

Thank you, sister, you were a friend,
Though that was long ago
You opened a door that changed my life
More than you will ever know

You were a friend way back when
With bagels and cream cheese
And spiced tea at midnight
When you shared your world with me…

Sister-Woman Friends

Who are the friends I hold most dear?
And drive crazy with all this stuff?
Always springing a poem on them
And reading them my junk?

Over cell phone signals all jacked up
In my car, asking for their local news
Our voices echo as I idle in the park
And fish around for their good reviews

They are my sister-women
And stronger than most men
To go through this with me for many years
Afraid it will not end

I lift their names to heaven's gate
Petitioning for their sanity
And asking God to bless their lives
The way they have blessed me

Though our phones don't coordinate
(Maybe she fears a poem attack)
We text and talk on messenger
Martha always has my back

Sharon, well, you know she knows
My schizophrenic ways
And has stuck with me all my life
Since her monolingual days

Cheryl endures my writing madness
More than people know
She actually helps me like an editor
Get reality to each word on every row

Then there's Debbie, what a champ
Cheers each word from pen or mouth
And because she drew the Texas straw
Helps me navigate around my house

Dortha Shirley, what can I say?
She cheers for the writer in me
Encourages, inspires, just like long ago
She grants this student much dignity

Lorelle, of Down Under, tops the charts
I owe her my highest praise
She kept me from quitting Oxford
And coached me on to higher grades

There's an Oxford diploma on my wall
Of which each of these ladies had a part
And if a book ever rolls off the press
I thank them with all my heart

The Sister-women invested their time
And hearts and ears in me
Cheered me on and kept me calm
Seeing what I couldn't see

They helped me stay on my path
Provoking an authentic version of me
Pushing me to reach my dream
Regardless of being sixty

Oxford's on my chest, wall, and hand
Books whisper in the wind
But the best things I got from Oxford?
Are my Sister-Women friends

Reflections

I peek at myself in the mirror
In a book of poetry
An anthology of who I was,
Am, and plan to be

I step back into the past
Indulge in memory
Of those I loved, forgot, forgave
For all they were to me

Some were losses, some were gains
Some helped me to endure
And some cluttered up my life
With loads of their manure

I learned from all the scallywags
Both here and across the sea
Their devastating impact resulted
In a stronger, wiser me

The brother, sister, sinner friends
Brought out the best in me
Pointed to a higher plane
For me to live and be

Childhood musings recall
The blessings of my birth
Vespers sought forgiveness
Exploring pain and all its worth

Losses, recovery, and of all my gains
The sweetest friends on Earth
Come flooding back between the lines
Ring out from all the words

Some losses were my own fault
Not all the gains my own
Darkness brought relief from heat
And guided me back home

I can't go back to yesteryear
Kissing all the frogs
Digging up my past
Or resurrect my dogs

But memories make me stronger
Shine light to guide my day
Leaving dangers far behind
They help me find my way

Perhaps my musings help a friend
Who's climbing to the light
Give courage to endure their pain
If I chose the words just right

At the break of each new day
I'll seek to shine my light
Cut myself a little slack
Then sleep in peace at night

I celebrate my scallywags, lovers,
Brothers, sisters, sinners, friends
May each new day rise like a prayer
As our lives begin again

Holy Edit

Lord God whose words brought order
And granted each heart light
Whose holy book blesses souls
And changes wrongs to right

Bless the words that fall on this page
The lines where thoughts abide
May they help another know
You're always on their side

And bless those bitter scallywags
Who came out in my tale
Who hated themselves more than me
And knew better, good and well

Watch over the friends we left
And the ones who ran on ahead
And forgive us all our trespasses
Go easy on our dead

For you spoke your words into the void
And brought forth good and light
Gave man a sun to guide his day
And stars to light his night

I humbly approach your throne
Asking you to edit me
Straighten up my jumbled heart
Delete what needs to delete

Speak and bring forth order
Edit all our speech
Help our hearts align with yours
Grant us rest and peace

Enough

There is a world out there
It waits to see
what I decide to do with me

Will I be brave
Or hide in here
And bury my words beneath despair

Or will I dare
To seek the light
And shine my words into the night

And shatter darkness
Into day
Help others run demons away

And rise back up
When fallen low
To show the lost which way to go

They say it takes just one small word
Echoed forth
To save the world

I doubt it's simple as they say

But if now and then
It works that way

Then maybe something
Falling from my pen
Will help another now and then

And if that's all
My words make of this stuff
Blessing another will be enough

Printed in the USA
CPSIA information can be obtained
at www.ICGtesting.com
LVHW011303121024
793574LV00065B/1262